American Moments

ABDO
Daughters

THE 2000
PRESIDENTIAL ELECTION

By Cory Gunderson

VISIT US AT
WWW.ABDOPUB.COM

Published by ABDO Publishing Company, 4940 Viking Drive, Suite 622, Edina, Minnesota 55435. Copyright ©2004 by Abdo Consulting Group, Inc. International copyrights reserved in all countries. No part of this book may be reproduced in any form without written permission from the publisher.

Printed in the United States.

Edited by: Sheila Rivera
Contributing Editor: Jessica Klein
Cover Design: Mighty Media
Interior Design and Production: Terry Dunham Incorporated
Photos: Corbis, Department of Defense, Library of Congress

Library of Congress Cataloging-in-Publication Data

Gunderson, Cory Gideon.
    The 2000 presidential election / Cory Gunderson.
        p. cm. -- (American moments)
    Summary: Discusses the people and events of the controversial 2000 presidential election, the results of which were not decided until over one month after election day.
    Includes bibliographical references (p.) and index.
    Contents: History repeats itself -- The candidates -- The election -- No clear winner -- Not out of the woods yet -- Addressing the issues.
    ISBN 1-59197-284-1
    1. Presidents--United States--Election--2000--Juvenile literature. 2. Presidential candidates--United States--History--20th century--Juvenile literature. 3. United States--Politics and government--1993-2001--Juvenile literature. [1. Presidents--Election--2000. 2. Elections. 3. United States--Politics and government--1993-2001.] I. Title. II. Series.

E889.G86 2003
324.973'0929--dc21
                                                    2003048134

CONTENTS

HISTORY REPEATS ITSELF

American citizens voted on November 7, 2000, for the man they wanted to be president. They expected to wake the next morning knowing who had won the election. Instead, the nation watched as the media and political experts struggled to determine the election's winner.

It took 36 days of recounts and court battles to determine the winner. The 2000 presidential election was one of the most controversial in U.S. history. Yet it was not the first election like this.

In 1824, John Quincy Adams ran against Andrew Jackson, William H. Crawford, and Henry Clay for the presidency. No candidate received the required majority of electoral votes. This meant that the House of Representatives had to determine the winner. Each state's representative got one vote.

Henry Clay was Kentucky's representative and Speaker of the House. Clay's state legislature ordered him to vote for Andrew

John Quincy Adams

Jackson. But Clay disliked Jackson. Clay had taken last place in the election against Adams, Crawford, and Jackson. In a controversial move, Clay cast his state's vote for Adams.

After the election, a victorious Adams named Clay secretary of state. This angered many Jackson loyalists. They felt that Clay and Adams had made an unfair deal with one another. This criticism made the next years of both Adams's and Clay's political lives difficult.

Henry Clay

Another controversial election took place in 1876. This election was between Republican Rutherford B. Hayes and Democrat Samuel J. Tilden. Even though Tilden won the popular vote, the election wasn't decided. There were disagreements regarding which candidate won the most votes in South Carolina, Louisiana, and Florida. In order to decide the election, Congress appointed a 15-member electoral commission. The commission was to vote on who won the election. All eight Republicans on the commission believed that Hayes had won. The seven Democrats believed that Tilden was the election's winner. With a tight 8-7 vote, Hayes became the next president of the United States.

The 1888 election was controversial as well. This election pitted Democratic president Grover Cleveland against Republican senator Benjamin Harrison. Cleveland defeated Harrison in the popular vote.

Did You Know?

Grover Cleveland

Benjamin Harrison

Grover Cleveland's wedding

- Grover Cleveland was elected U.S. president in 1884.

- Cleveland was defeated by Benjamin Harrison in 1888.

- Cleveland was reelected four years later in 1892.

- Grover Cleveland was the only U.S. president to leave office and return for a second term four years later.

- Grover Cleveland was also the only U.S. president to get married in the White House.

- The Baby Ruth candy bar was named after president Cleveland's daughter Ruth.

- Cleveland's daughter Esther was the first child born in the White House.

- Benjamin Harrison's grandfather was William Henry Harrison, the ninth president.

He had 5,540,050 votes to Harrison's 5,444,337. Despite these totals, Harrison received 233 electoral college votes and Cleveland received 168.

The presidential election of 2000 was similar to the election of 1888. The candidates in the 2000 election were Democrat Al Gore and Republican George W. Bush. Gore received 50,996,116 popular votes and Bush received 50,456,169. The race was too close to call. A tally of each state's electoral votes was necessary to determine the winner.

Unfortunately, Florida's election results were unclear. Its popular vote count could not be determined, and its electoral votes were debated for 36 days. In the end, the state of Florida tipped the balance in Bush's favor. Bush received 271 electoral votes. Al Gore received 266.

The 2000 presidential election resulted in a victory for Bush. The confusion it caused illustrated the need to reform the presidential election process.

Even though Al Gore received more popular votes, George W. Bush won the 2000 election.

Vice President Al Gore and Texas governor George W. Bush faced off in three debates before election day.

Bush's lead over Gore in the polls was slim. Each candidate used the debates to show why he should be elected to the presidency.

Bush presented himself as a leader who could work with Republicans and Democrats. Gore presented himself as someone who would fight for middle-class families.

The candidates spent most of their time debating topics such as education, Social Security, and health care.

THE CANDIDATES

GEORGE W. BUSH

George Walker Bush was born on July 6, 1946, in New Haven, Connecticut. He is the oldest child of former U.S. president George H.W. Bush and Barbara Bush. Bush has three brothers, Neil, Jeb, and Marvin. He also has a sister, Dorothy. Another sister, Robin, died in 1953 at age three. She died from leukemia, a bone marrow disease.

Bush was raised in Midland and Houston, Texas. Like his father, Bush attended Phillips Academy in Andover, Massachusetts. He

Neil   Jeb   Barbara   George W. Bush

George H.W. Bush   Marvin

Nicky

Dorothy

received his bachelor's degree in history from Yale University in 1968. Then he served as an F-102 fighter pilot in the Texas Air National Guard. In 1975, he earned a master of business administration from Harvard University.

In 1977, Bush founded an oil and gas company, which he named Arbusto. That same year, he married Laura Welch, a former librarian at Dawson Elementary School in Texas. Then in 1978, Bush ran for U.S. Congress. He lost the election, and returned to his oil company. He changed the company's name to Bush Exploration in 1981. Bush was the chief executive officer, or CEO, of this company. Soon the Bushes had twin girls. They named them Jenna and Barbara, after the girls' grandmothers.

Bush left the private sector in 1988 to work on his father's presidential campaign. Afterward, Bush brought together a group of people who bought the Texas Rangers baseball team. He was one of the team's managing partners for only a couple of years.

Bush returned to the political ring in 1994 when he ran for governor of Texas. He won the election by defeating popular Democratic incumbent Ann Richards. Bush won reelection in 1998. Shortly afterward, he announced he would run for the presidency as the Republican Party candidate.

Bush selected Wyoming native Richard B. Cheney as his running mate. Dick Cheney

George W. Bush and his running mate Dick Cheney

married his high school sweetheart, Lynne Ann Vincent, in 1964. The couple had two daughters, Elizabeth and Mary. Cheney had a long, prosperous political career.

In 1969, Cheney joined former President Richard Nixon's administration. When Gerald Ford became president in 1974, Cheney was a member of his administration. In November 1975, he became assistant to the president and White House chief of staff.

When Ford left the White House, Cheney returned to Wyoming. He was elected that state's lone congressman in the House of Representatives in 1977. He won reelection five times in a row. Cheney served as chairman on the Republican Policy Committee from 1981 to 1987. He became House minority whip the next year. When George H.W. Bush became president in 1988, Cheney served as his secretary of defense.

AL GORE

Albert Gore Jr. was born in Washington DC on March 31, 1948. He was the second of two children born to former U.S. congressman Albert Gore Sr. and Pauline Gore. Gore had a sister, Nancy, who died of lung cancer in 1984. She was 45 years old. In addition to Washington DC, Gore was also raised in Carthage, Tennessee.

Gore attended St. Albans Episcopal School in Washington DC. He graduated from Harvard University in 1969 with high honors and a degree in government. After graduating, Gore went into military service. In 1970 he married Elizabeth Mary "Tipper" Aitcheson. They would later have four children, Karenna, Kristin, Sarah, and Albert III.

Gore spent a couple of months in Vietnam working as an army reporter. He returned home in 1971 and began working as a reporter

Al Gore, with wife Tipper, at a New Mexico presidential campaign rally

for the *Nashville Tennessean* newspaper. While working at the *Tennessean*, Gore studied at Vanderbilt University Divinity School. He enrolled in Vanderbilt University Law School in 1974 and moved into politics a short time later. In 1976, he won his first election as a Tennessee representative. He served four terms in the House. In 1984, he ran for the U.S. Senate and won.

Gore made his first bid for the White House in 1988. He lost the primary election to Michael Dukakis. In 1992, Bill Clinton selected Senator Gore as his running mate for the presidential election. The pair won that year and was reelected in 1996. In 2000, Gore ran for the White House again. This time he ran as the Democratic candidate for president.

Gore's running mate for the 2000 presidential election was Connecticut senator Joseph Lieberman. Lieberman was born in Stamford, Connecticut, on February 24, 1942. He received his bachelor's degree from Yale in 1964. Three years later, he received a law degree from Yale Law School.

Lieberman was first elected to the Connecticut state Senate in 1970. He served there for 10 years. For six of those years, he was majority leader. He returned to private legal practice in 1980 and remained there for only two years. From 1982 to 1988, Lieberman served as Connecticut's twenty-first attorney general.

In 1988, Lieberman left this post to become a U.S. senator. He was elected three times and retained his senatorial seat after the 2000 election. Lieberman lives in New Haven, Connecticut, and Washington DC with his wife, Hadassah. The couple has four children, Matthew, Rebecca, Ethan, and Hana.

Opposite page: *Bill Clinton and his running mate Al Gore celebrate their victory in the 1992 presidential election.*

Republican Party

THE REPUBLICAN PARTY TYPICALLY:

Focuses on the power of the people to make change.

Believes that if the government leaves businesses alone, everybody benefits.

Supports free trade.

Favors lower taxes.

Supports equal rights and opportunities for everybody.

An elephant, like the one shown here, is commonly used as a symbol for the Republican Party.

Democratic Party

THE DEMOCRATIC PARTY TYPICALLY:

Focuses on the power of the government to make change.

Believes that the government should make sure that businesses are being fair.

Supports workers' rights.

Favors letting the government use tax money to support programs that need it most.

Supports equal rights and opportunities for everybody.

A donkey is often used to represent the Democratic Party. This symbol was unofficially adopted in 1828.

THE
ELECTION

Bush and Gore were not the only candidates to run in the 2000 presidential election. They represented the two major parties, but other candidates also competed. The other candidates did not draw a large percentage of the vote. They did, however, draw plenty of attention.

Ralph Nader was the Green Party candidate. This party was created in 1984. At the time, it was called the Committees of Correspondence. The Green Party works to "harmonize society with nature and harmonize human with human."

Nader was born in Winsted, Connecticut, in 1934. He is the son of Lebanese immigrants Rose and Nathra Nader. In 1955, he graduated with honors from Princeton University. He graduated from Harvard Law School in 1958.

Nader first publicly announced his role as a consumer advocate, or watchdog, in April 1959. He wrote the article "The Safe Car You Can't Buy." It was published in the *Nation* magazine. The article discussed the ways in which automobiles are built for human convenience and luxury, rather than for safety. This article launched Nader's career.

The then-29-year-old attorney left Connecticut and moved to Washington DC. While there, Nader worked as a consultant for the

Ralph Nader continued his commitment to consumer advocacy when he wrote Unsafe at Any Speed in 1965. In the book, Nader claimed that American automakers were compromising safety for profits. As a result, Congress held hearings on auto safety, and the Highway Safety Act and National Traffic and Motor Vehicle Safety Act were passed in 1966. These laws allowed the government to legislate safety standards for automobiles.

www.voteNader.org

U.S. Department of Labor. He also wrote articles for the *Nation* and the *Christian Science Monitor*.

Nader helped create the modern consumer movement. Like-minded thinkers were invited to come to Washington DC and join Nader's cause. In 1971, Nader created an organization called Public Citizen. Its goal was to protect Washington DC consumers. Today, more than 150,000 people are involved with the organization. Nader left Public Citizen in 1980 to devote his time to lecturing, book writing, and politics.

Patrick Buchanan was another major presidential candidate in 2000. He ran as a member of the Reform Party. The Reform Party seeks to change the way the government operates. It is dedicated to financial responsibility, political accountability, and the election of ethical officials.

Buchanan was born on November 2, 1938, in Washington DC. He received a bachelor's degree from Georgetown

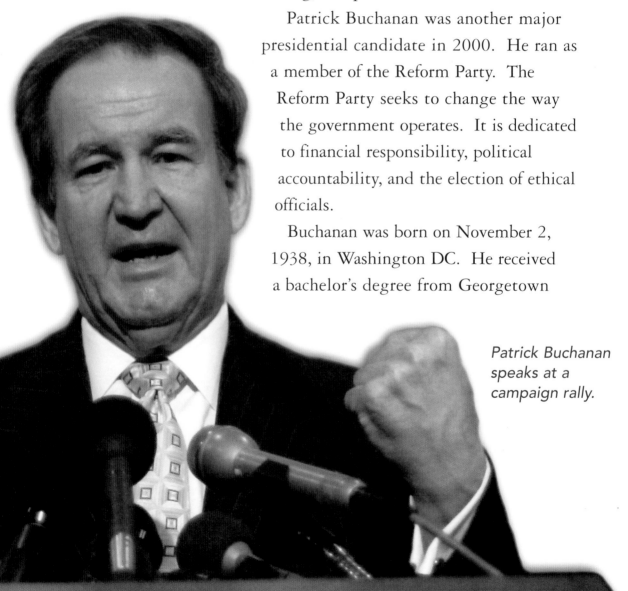

Patrick Buchanan speaks at a campaign rally.

University in 1961. In 1962, he received his master's in journalism from Columbia University.

That year Buchanan began his professional career as a writer. He was the youngest editorial writer in the country to work for a major newspaper. Buchanan entered politics in 1966, when he worked as an assistant to Richard Nixon. At that time, Nixon was a presidential hopeful. Buchanan then worked as a speechwriter for President Nixon from 1969 to 1974. He also worked as communications director for President Ronald Reagan from 1985 to 1987. Buchanan himself was a presidential candidate in 1992 and 1996. In between roles in politics, Buchanan works as a columnist and media commentator.

The presence of these two additional candidates made an already tight race even closer. A number of opinion polls were conducted in the months prior to the race. Two months before the election, one poll showed Bush and Gore to be within 1 percentage point of each other. Bush held a 1 percent margin in the opinion poll on election day.

Americans went to the polls to vote on November 7, 2000. Because the states on the East Coast are in the earliest time zone, those citizens were first to vote. Their results were the first to be counted. The total number of popular votes would determine which candidate would win each state's electoral votes.

OPINION POLLS

In an opinion poll, a media representative asks a variety of people whom they plan to vote for in an upcoming election. Journalists view these results as indicators as to who might win the election.

As early as 1824, two newspapers relied on opinion polls to determine the public's view of political candidates. These papers were the *Harrisburg Pennsylvanian* and the *Raleigh Star*.

As the election progressed, both Gore and Bush won many electoral votes. Gore won many states in the East, including Maine, New York, Rhode Island, and Massachusetts. Meanwhile, Bush won many of the states in the South, including Alabama, Georgia, and Texas.

Political analysts knew that Gore would win large states such as California and New York. These states have a history of voting for Democrats. Analysts believed that if Gore could win the three big swing states, he would win the election. The three swing states were Michigan, Pennsylvania, and Florida.

The people, thus the Electoral College, in swing states might vote Democrat or Republican. These states could "swing" either way from one year to the next. These states are unlike many other states, which typically vote for candidates from the same political party consistently over the years.

Early in the evening on election day, the media reported that Gore had won all three swing states. With these states' electoral votes, it appeared that he was going to be the next president of the United States.

More vote totals came in from across the country. Florida's vote total changed throughout the night. Bush seemed to be gaining momentum. It appeared that the media had made a mistake in saying Gore had won Florida. It was beginning to look as though he hadn't won the state after all.

By the time all states had closed their polls, Gore had won 266 electoral votes. Bush had received 246. A candidate needs at least 270 electoral votes to win an election. This meant that the candidate who received Florida's 25 votes would be the winner.

Early on the morning of November 8, the media said that Bush had won Florida. This meant he also won the election. Gore believed he would likely lose to Bush by 50,000 votes. He called Bush to concede the election around 2:15 AM eastern standard time.

As Florida's ballot counting continued, Bush's lead began to drop. Soon election officials said that the race was too close to call. Gore called Bush back 45 minutes after his first call. This time Gore withdrew his concession. He told Bush he was not giving up.

At 4:15 AM, the press took back its statement as well. It no longer knew if Bush was the winner. Neither candidate had enough electoral votes to win the presidency.

U.S. citizens cast their votes.

ELECTORAL VOTES

This map shows the number of electoral votes each state had in the 2000 election.

In the 2000 presidential election, the states with the fewest number of electoral votes included: Alaska, Delaware, District of Columbia, Montana, North Dakota, South Dakota, Vermont, and Wyoming.

California had 54 electoral votes, more than any other state.

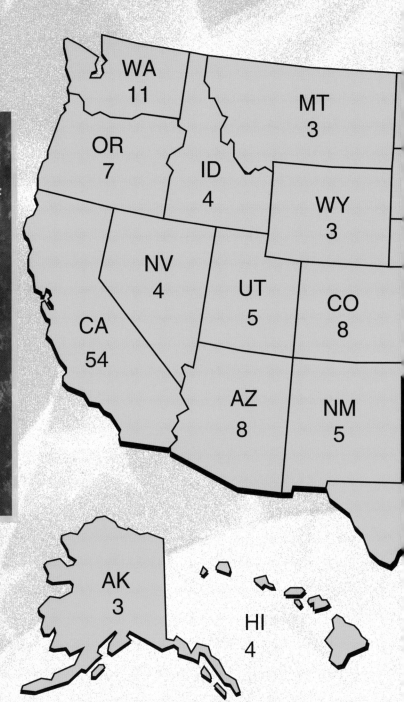

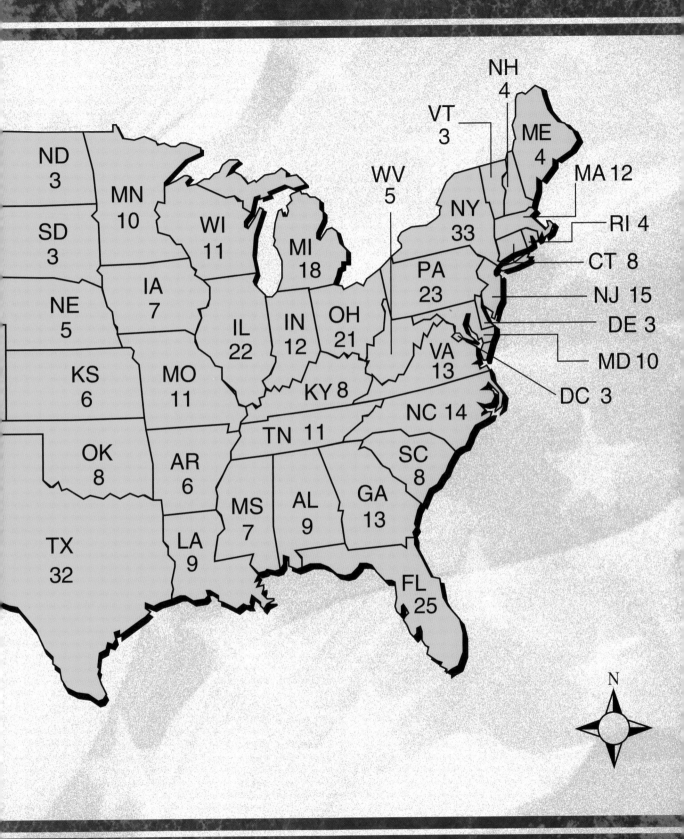

NO CLEAR WINNER

Florida ballots were counted. Bush led Gore by fewer than 2,000 votes. While Bush was listed as the winner of this pivotal state, the votes had to be recounted. Florida's law required a ballot recount in counties where Bush had won by less than .5 percent. All 67 Florida counties had to recount their votes.

The votes were run through the machines again. These machines tallied votes. Bush's lead shrunk significantly. Gore's supporters argued that the machine recount was not fair. They believed that the machines had not produced an accurate count. The machines couldn't read punch cards that weren't completely punched out. Gore's supporters believed only a hand count of the votes could accurately tell the difference. By this time, the Associated Press (AP) estimated that Bush's lead had shrunk to a mere 327 votes.

In several counties, the machines were unable to correctly read all of the ballots. Confusion grew in Palm Beach County. There were a surprisingly large number of votes for Buchanan. Many voters said the butterfly ballots they had used were confusing. Some said they had voted for Buchanan accidentally. They had meant to vote for Gore.

A butterfly ballot opens like a book and has candidates' names on each side. Arrows point from each candidate's name to the center of the ballot. Voters were to punch the hole that lined up with their

THE BUTTERFLY BALLOT

In Palm Beach, Florida, the butterfly ballot caused voters great confusion in the 2000 election. When voters use the butterfly ballot, they punch out a hole next to the name of the candidate they wish to elect. Many voters realized that they had made a mistake in casting their vote and tried to correct their ballots. More than 19,000 ballots were disqualified because the ballot sheets were punched twice.

Teresa LePore, Palm Beach elections supervisor, designed the butterfly ballot. She wanted to make sure that Palm Beach's elderly voters could read the ballot. She decided that the two-page butterfly ballot allowed for each candidate's name to be listed in large type. If the names were listed on just one page, the type would be smaller and more difficult to read.

On the 2000 ballots, Democrats were listed second in the left column, but they were the third hole on the ballot. This confused many voters.

In the future, Palm Beach voters will use special computers with touch screens to cast their votes. The computers will not let citizens vote for two candidates. Each will display a reminder of which candidate was voted for and allow voters to correct their vote if necessary. Palm Beach election officials and citizens hope to avoid the ballot problems that they experienced in the 2000 presidential election.

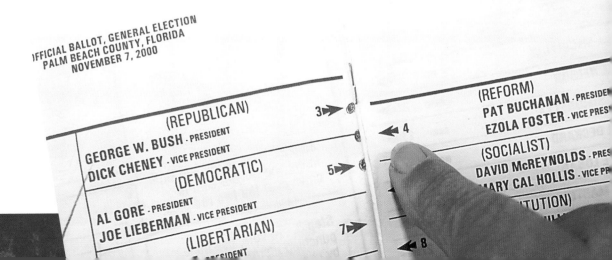

chosen candidate's name. Many people did not understand the order in which the candidates were listed. They said they accidentally voted for a candidate they did not support.

More than 19,000 voters in Palm Beach County had punched out spaces for two different presidential candidates. Officials believed that these people had punched a second time to correct their first choice. These votes were not counted. This only added to the election controversy.

Because of these ballot problems, Democrats asked for hand recounts in four counties. These counties included Palm Beach, Miami-Dade, Broward, and Volusia. On November 12, Palm Beach officials voted to conduct a total hand recount of the presidential ballots. Within two weeks, the other three counties had begun recounts.

The Republicans protested these recounts for several reasons. They stated there were no laws governing hand recounts. They didn't believe election officials could accurately determine a citizen's intended vote. Some Republicans were also concerned that the Democratic election officials could cheat during the recounts in favor of Gore.

Boxes were set up at the LeRoy Collins Leon County Public Library to prepare for the manual recount of Miami-Dade ballots.

Because of these issues, both Bush and Gore hired their own legal teams. The Bush team was the first to file a suit in federal district court. On November 11, Bush's team asked to stop the recounts. A federal judge rejected that request on November 13.

Meanwhile, there were absentee ballots to consider. Florida's deadline for counting absentee ballots was November 14. Voters who cannot make it to their polling places on election day mail in absentee ballots. On November 13, Florida secretary of state Katherine Harris said she wouldn't extend the November 14 deadline past 5:00 PM, except for ballots received from overseas. The deadline for those was extended to midnight on November 17.

On November 14, Palm Beach County decided to temporarily stop its recount. Miami-Dade County decided to limit its recount to about 1 percent of its votes. Harris asked the counties to explain why they felt they deserved a recount.

She was not satisfied with the counties' reasoning. On November 15, she asked the

Florida secretary of state Katherine Harris

Florida Supreme Court to stop all of the recounts. AP reported that Bush's margin of victory had shrunk to 286 votes.

On November 16, Bush's team went to court a second time, again trying to stop the recounts. This time the case went to a federal court of appeals. Gore's team made a motion in this court the same day. It wanted to stop Harris's certification of Florida's votes. Also on November 16, the Florida Supreme Court ruled that Palm Beach County could continue its recounts.

The federal court of appeals ruled against Bush on November 17. The same day, the Florida Supreme Court ruled that Harris couldn't certify the Florida votes until the court could review Gore's motion. The hearing was scheduled for November 20. At this time, Miami-Dade and Palm Beach counties both proceeded with their manual recounts.

On November 18, the overseas absentee ballots were counted. AP estimated that Bush's lead had increased to 930 votes. On November 21, the Florida Supreme Court ruled that all hand counts already underway could continue. The court gave the counties until November 26 to complete them. The Bush team mounted an appeal to the U.S. Supreme Court. The Court agreed to hear the appeal on November 24.

Miami-Dade County stopped its recounts on November 23. County officials didn't believe they would be able to finish before the deadline. On November 26, Harris certified the results. But Palm Beach County's ballots weren't included, because they had missed the deadline by two hours. The certification made Bush the next U.S. president. He won by 537 votes.

NOT OUT OF THE WOODS YET

Bush and Gore continued to battle in the courts. Gore's legal team had asked that a Florida state circuit court order a hand recount of about 13,000 undervotes in particular counties.

An undervote occurs when the machine reads the ballot incorrectly and registers that no vote has been cast. In contrast, an overvote occurs when the machine reads the ballot incorrectly and registers that the voter cast more than one vote.

Circuit court judge N. Sanders Sauls dealt the Gore team a difficult blow. On December 4, Judge Sauls ruled that a recount would not be granted. Gore appealed this decision to the Florida Supreme Court.

On December 8, 2000, the Florida Supreme Court voted 4-3 in favor of manual recounts in every county with large numbers of undervotes. The Bush team countered with an appeal to the U.S. Supreme Court. The team stated that the recount was illegal, based on the Fourteenth Amendment. This amendment to the Constitution states that every individual must be treated equally. On December 9, the judges stopped the manual recounts. The U.S. Supreme Court scheduled a hearing on the issue for December 11.

Opposite page: Circuit court judge N. Sanders Sauls is a registered Democrat. He denied Gore's request for a recount.

George W. Bush takes the oath of
office as he is sworn in as president

Gore was running out of time. The electoral votes would be cast on December 12. If Gore could not convince the judges to support a recount, Bush would become the next president. Gore knew that if the election was not decided by December 12, then Florida's legislature would decide who received that state's electoral votes. This would most likely mean victory for Bush, as the majority of Florida's legislature was Republican.

The lengthy court battle finally ended on December 12. The Supreme Court judges determined that, based on the Fourteenth Amendment, a state's laws had to be applied to everyone in the same way. They knew that not all counties had time to conduct recounts. They also knew some votes were going to be hand counted and some would be machine counted. If the court granted the recounts, different standards would be applied to different counties. This would mean that not every person was being treated equally. So the justices of the Supreme Court ruled 5-4 that the recounts were unconstitutional.

This news was devastating for Gore because it meant his battle was over. On December 13, he called and officially conceded the election to Bush. Even though Gore had won the popular vote, with 50,996,116 votes to Bush's 50,456,169 votes, he still lost the election.

The electoral votes were counted on January 5, 2001. Bush had 271 electoral votes while Gore had 266. Gore was the first presidential candidate to win the popular vote and lose the election since Grover Cleveland in 1888. George W. Bush became the forty-third president of the United States. He was sworn in on January 20, 2001.

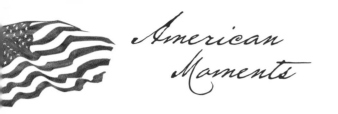
American Moments

ADDRESSING THE ISSUES

CHANGES IN FLORIDA

The problematic election of 2000 prompted several changes to the election process. These changes were designed to make voting easier and more accurate. Officials hoped the will of the people would be better represented in the future.

The majority of the election 2000 problems occurred in Florida. So on May 9, 2001, the state created its own legislation to prevent future difficulties. This legislation was called the Florida Election Reform Act of 2001, or FERA.

One of the first issues that FERA addressed concerned ballot chads. Chads are the small pieces of paper that voters punched through ballots to indicate their candidate choice. The machines that count the votes often had trouble reading ballots that contained chads that were not pushed through perfectly. FERA ruled that punch card ballots could no longer be used in Florida. Instead, more foolproof ballots would be used. The FERA panel suggested that counties that could afford them switch to touch screen voting booths, because they resulted in fewer errors.

Another change addressed the issue of relocating citizens. Before the 2000 election, registered citizens of one district who moved out of that district had to reregister to vote in their new district. This was

*Judge Robert Rosenberg uses a magnifying glass
to determine if this ballot contains a dangling chad.*

true even if they moved within the same county. New legislation said that citizens who moved into a new district within the same county did not have to reregister to vote.

The FERA bill also worked to correct the wrongs that many African Americans said they experienced. Many of these citizens believed that poll workers discriminated against them and cast their votes aside. The new FERA legislation prevented poll workers from discarding ballots.

FERA also attempted to remove all restrictions on absentee ballot voting. In the past, Florida citizens needed to cite the reason they wanted to vote absentee. These reasons could have included illness,

Jesse Jackson, a long-time advocate for African-American rights, leads a crowd of protesters in Palm Beach, Florida.

Governor Jeb Bush authorized the Florida Election Reform Act of 2001.

military service, or other obstacles. But the new law allowed any Florida citizen to cast an absentee ballot, regardless of reason.

One of the major conflicts of the 2000 election was the debate regarding election deadlines. The Republicans believed that the deadlines previously established should be enforced. They felt the election should have been resolved by mid-December as others had.

The Democrats argued that the deadlines didn't leave enough time for recounts. The FERA panel extended the deadline for ballot certification by four extra days. It hoped that this was enough time for future election officials to resolve any problems that may arise.

CHANGES ACROSS THE NATION

Florida wasn't the only state where elections faced a serious overhaul. Across the nation, a nonpolitical task force of election professionals was created. This group was called the Election Center Task Force. It offered its own suggestions for reshaping voting in the country. The task force recommended national standards for voting processes and equipment. Uniform standards would make it easier to interpret a voter's true intent. It offered guidelines for choosing what is a valid marking on a ballot. This system would also help states prevent duplicate voter registrations across the country.

The Election Center Task Force suggested that election day employees' skills be improved. This meant spending additional government money to train those who worked the polls. It also meant paying these employees higher salaries.

39

In addition, the task force believed that registration deadlines and poll locations should be listed on all voting literature. The center also supported early absentee voting and voting rights for pardoned felons. Rules were put in place to stop the media from predicting an election earlier than 11:00 PM eastern standard time. Finally, the U.S. Department of Justice was put in charge of investigating any claims of unfairness during an election.

On October 16, 2002, the U.S. Senate approved a bill called the Help America Vote Act. It includes several new measures, such as additional public education regarding voting and the replacement of outdated voting machines. The bill also gives voters the freedom to correct any mistakes they make in casting their votes. In addition, a temporary ballot is provided if a voter's eligibility is in doubt. The ballot is counted only if eligibility is determined.

The act also requires all first time voters to present a valid driver's license. Those who don't have a driver's license can still vote. They must, however, tell an election official the last four digits of their Social Security number. The bill also provides voting machines for disabled voters. On October 29, 2002, George W. Bush signed the Help America Vote Act into law.

Election 2000 was one of the most contested elections ever to take place. It was also a defining moment in American history. For the first time, the U.S. Supreme Court was involved in an election decision. Election laws and the U.S. Constitution were questioned. In the end, the controversy caused by this historic election changed the way Americans vote.

The Help America Vote Act was passed to prevent election problems, such as those that occurred during the 2000 presidential election.

TIMELINE

 Nov. 7 2000 U.S. citizens vote to elect the forty-third president.

 Nov. 8 2000 The news media declares Bush the winner. Gore concedes to Bush, but later withdraws his concession.

 Nov. 11 2000 George W. Bush's legal team files a suit to prevent the hand counting of ballots. The team is defeated.

 Nov. 17 2000 The Florida Supreme Court tells Katherine Harris she cannot certify Florida's election results.

 Nov. 21 2000 The Florida Supreme Court orders the hand counting of ballots to continue. The deadline for counting is extended to November 26.

 Nov. 26 2000 Harris certifies Florida's vote. Bush is declared the winner of Florida.

 Dec. 8 2000 The Florida Supreme Court orders a recount of the undervotes in those Florida counties where it has not already occurred.

Dec. 9 2000 The U.S. Supreme Court rules that the recount of undervotes be stopped.

 Dec. 12 2000 The U.S. Supreme Court rules the recounts unconstitutional.

 Dec. 13 2000 Al Gore concedes the election.

 Jan. 5 2001 Congress counts the electoral votes.

 Jan. 20 2001 George W. Bush becomes the forty-third president of the United States.

 May 9 2001 Florida governor Jeb Bush authorizes the Florida Election Reform Act of 2001.

American Moments

FAST FACTS

The Reform Party gained national attention in the 1990s when Ross Perot ran for U.S. president as a Reform Party candidate.

Joseph Lieberman was the first Jewish nominee for U.S. vice president.

Polls on the East Coast are the first to open on election day and the first to close.

In recent presidential elections, the winning candidate has had to have at least 270 electoral votes.

In the 2000 election, 51 percent of Americans of voting age cast ballots in the presidential race. American Citizens must be at least 18 years old to vote.

In 1996, Massachusetts banned the butterfly ballot. Vote-counting machines sometimes had trouble counting these ballots accurately.

For decades, most Americans voted in a booth where they pulled a lever by a candidate's name. These mechanical lever voting machines are no longer made.

The 1960 election between John F. Kennedy and Richard Nixon was one of the closest presidential races in history. Kennedy won the popular vote count by less than 120,000 votes.

As the U.S. vice president at the time of the 2000 election, Al Gore certified the results of the Electoral College.

WEB SITES
WWW.ABDOPUB.COM

Would you like to learn more about the 2000 Presidential Election? Please visit **www.abdopub.com** to find up-to-date Web site links about the 2000 presidential election and other American moments. These links are routinely monitored and updated to provide the most current information available.

Democratic candidate Al Gore shakes hands with Republican candidate George W. Bush before their televised presidential debate.

GLOSSARY

absentee ballot: a ballot mailed to a polling place before an election. Voters who cannot travel to their polling place on election day vote by absentee ballot.

Associated Press (AP): a newsgathering organization.

chief of staff: a person who is responsible to the president of the United States.

Electoral College: the group that elects the president and vice president by casting electoral votes. When people vote for a president, the political party that gets the most votes in each state sends its representatives to the Electoral College. There, the representatives vote for their party's candidate.

eligible (eligibility): to qualify for something. For example, citizens must qualify for the right to vote.

House minority whip: the person from the minority party responsible for influencing the party's strategy on the floor of the House of Representatives.

House of Representatives: the lower house in the U.S. Congress. Citizens elect members of the House to make laws for the nation.

incumbent: the person currently holding a political office.

media: communication companies, such as newspapers, television, and radio.

pardoned felon: someone who is forgiven of a serious crime.

private sector: privately owned, as opposed to government-run, businesses.

secretary of state: a member of the president's or a governor's cabinet who handles relations with other countries or states.

Senate: the upper house in the U.S. Congress. Citizens elect members of the senate to make laws for the nation.

task force: a temporary grouping of people brought together to accomplish a specific goal.

Vietnam: a country in southeast Asia. The United States fought to keep North Vietnam from taking over South Vietnam in the Vietnam war from 1955 to 1975.

INDEX